Windows of Heaven
Art Glass, Doors & Motifs of LDS Temples
COLORING BOOK
VOLUME 1

JOSEPH CHRISTENSEN

SKYBEAST MEDIA
RIGBY, IDAHO

The drawings created for this book are inspired from the exterior windows, doors, stained glass, iron work, and other visual details and artistry found on and around temples of The Church of Jesus Christ of Latter-day Saints from across the world.

Just because the illustrations are inspired from real world references, doesn't mean you have to color them that way. No matter how you want to approach your coloring - the key is to relax and enjoy it. Have fun!

To help prevent color bleed and pressure lines from transferring to other pages, place a blank sheet of card stock underneath the page you are coloring.

Windows of Heaven: Art Glass, Doors & Motifs of LDS Temples
Coloring Book - Volume 1
Series: Choose the Bright - Straight and Narrow Paths to Color

This is an independent creative work.
Not an official publication of The Church of Jesus Christ of Latter-day Saints.

Trademarks are property of their respective owners.

Skybeast Media
books@skybeast.com

ISBN-13: 978-1546441526
ISBN-10: 1546441522

To my family
who fill in the empty spaces with color

facebook.com/ChoosetheBright

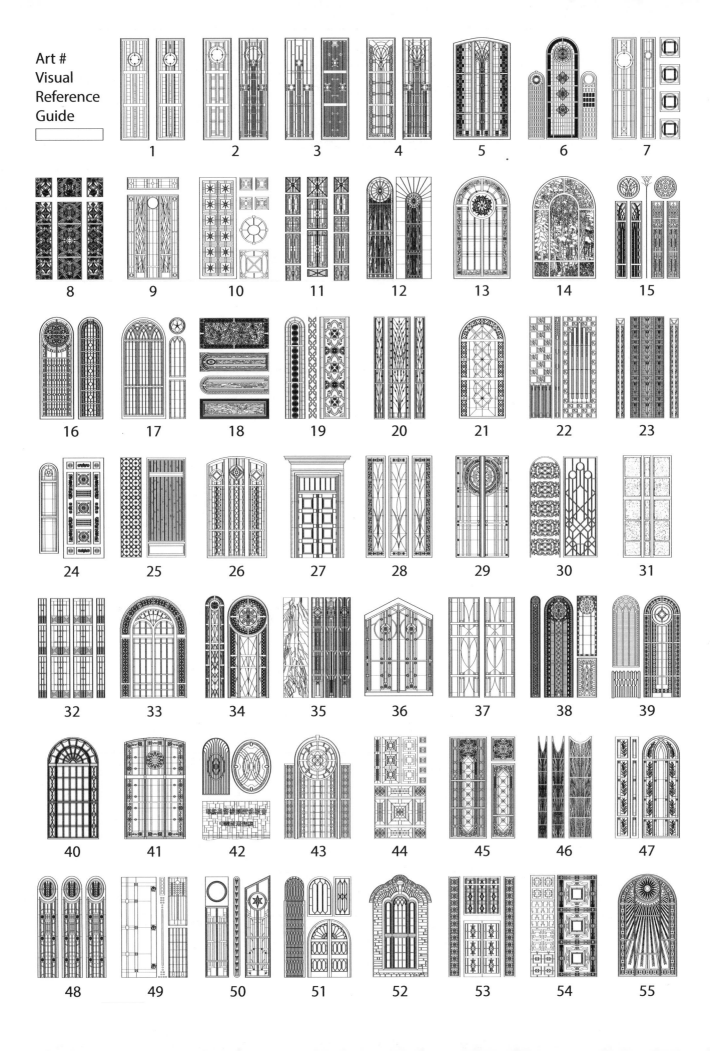

1   2   3   4   5   6   7

8   9   10   11   12   13   14   15

16   17   18   19   20   21   22   23

24   25   26   27   28   29   30   31

32   33   34   35   36   37   38   39

40   41   42   43   44   45   46   47

48   49   50   51   52   53   54   55

This book (Volume 1) primarily consists of drawings relating to temples listed A - L (Aba Nigeria Temple through Lubbock Texas Temple) using the city/area + state/country naming convention. Several temples outside of this alphabetical range are also included because of shared visual themes. Below is the index of temples listed by Art # with additional explanations of thematically grouped temples listed out of alphabetical order.

INDEX OF TEMPLES LISTED BY ART #:

#1-3 (Small Temples) In1998, President Gordon B. Hinckley announced the expansion of a program to construct "small, beautiful, serviceable temples" as a means of bringing the temple to the people. Although each temple is unique, many of these temples share common window glass and decorative iron work designs. These shared themes are divided into five categories which is detailed on the next page.

#4 Aba Nigeria and Asunción Paraguay Temples share stained glass window lead lines.

#5 Accra Ghana, #6 Albuquerque New Mexico

#7 Anchorage Alaska and Monticello Utah Temples. The tall narrow window configuration is shared between these two temples. Along with Colonia Juárez Chihuahua Mexico, these temples were a sort of pilot program to the small temples. It is evident that these windows and the circle in the square motif were precursors to the shared window designs (#1-3).

#8 Apia Samoa, #9 Atlanta Georgia

#10 Bern Switzerland, Hamilton New Zealand, Idaho Falls Idaho (#44) and Los Angeles California (#54) Temples all share a similar repeating square motif, but each is executed differently. The London England Temple (#53) also has a related repeating iron work design. The Stockholm Sweden and Johannesburg South Africa Temples have rounded design variants.

#11 Billings Montana, #12 Bogotá Colombia, #13-14 Boise Idaho, #15 Boston Massachusetts, #16 Bountiful Utah, #17 Brigham City Utah

#18 These window designs are realized through textural/dimensional shifts rather than color. The Brisbane Australia, Hong Kong China (#42) and Snowflake Arizona Temples have a similar organic texture surrounded by varied circular repeats. The Suva Fiji Temple has a floral central design and corner motifs with a stylized border.

#19 Buenos Aires Argentina, #20 Calgary Alberta, #21 Campinas Brazil, #22 Cardston Alberta, #23 Cebu City Philippines

#24 Cedar City Utah (window) and Cochabamba Bolivia (carved wood door). With the exception of the top circular designs, the spire windows of these two temples share very similar stained glass lead lines.

#25 Colonia Juárez Chihuahua Mexico and Oquirrh Mountain Utah Temple window designs use circles and stars. Similar to the windows in #18, the visuals are created by changes in materials, texture and dimension.

#26 Columbia River Washington, #27 Copenhagen Denmark, #28 Córdoba Argentina, #29 Curitiba Brazil

#30 Chicago Illinois and Dallas Texas Temples share the same geometric door design.

#31 Denver Colorado, #32 Draper Utah, #33 Fort Collins Colorado, #34 Fort Lauderdale Florida, #35 Frankfurt Germany and #35-36 Frieberg Germany, #37 The Gila Valley Arizona, #38 Gilbert Arizona, #39 Guatemala City Guatemala and Guayaquil Ecuador, #40 Hartford Connecticut, #41 Helsinki Finland, #42 Hong Kong China, #43 Houston Texas, #44 Idaho Falls Idaho, #45 Indianapolis Indiana, #46 Jordan River Utah, #47 Kansas City Missouri, #48 Kyiv Ukraine, #49 Laie Hawaii, #50 Las Vegas Nevada, #51 Lima Peru, #52 Logan Utah, #53 London England, #54 Los Angeles California, #55 Lubbock Texas

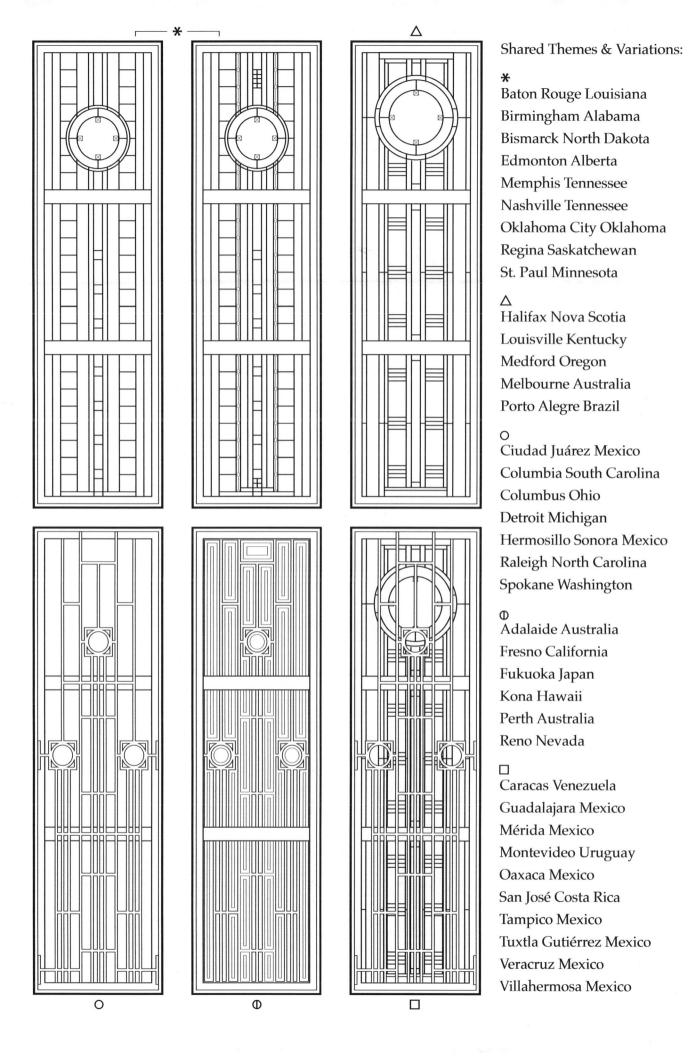

Shared Themes & Variations:

✳
Baton Rouge Louisiana
Birmingham Alabama
Bismarck North Dakota
Edmonton Alberta
Memphis Tennessee
Nashville Tennessee
Oklahoma City Oklahoma
Regina Saskatchewan
St. Paul Minnesota

△
Halifax Nova Scotia
Louisville Kentucky
Medford Oregon
Melbourne Australia
Porto Alegre Brazil

○
Ciudad Juárez Mexico
Columbia South Carolina
Columbus Ohio
Detroit Michigan
Hermosillo Sonora Mexico
Raleigh North Carolina
Spokane Washington

Φ
Adalaide Australia
Fresno California
Fukuoka Japan
Kona Hawaii
Perth Australia
Reno Nevada

□
Caracas Venezuela
Guadalajara Mexico
Mérida Mexico
Montevideo Uruguay
Oaxaca Mexico
San José Costa Rica
Tampico Mexico
Tuxtla Gutiérrez Mexico
Veracruz Mexico
Villahermosa Mexico

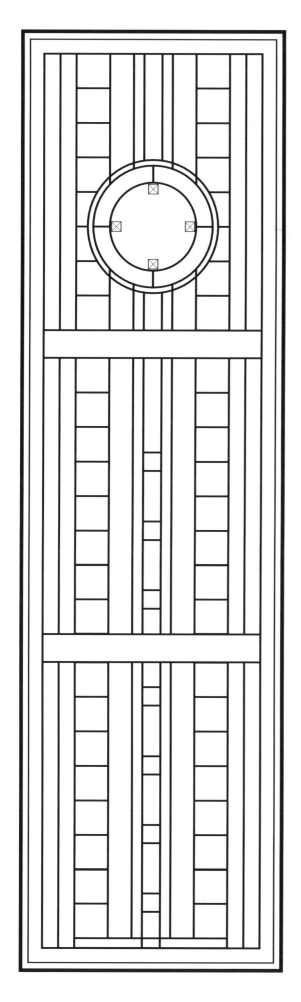 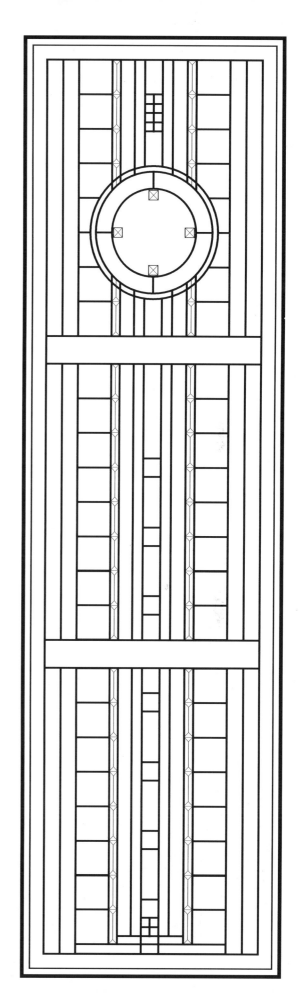

*

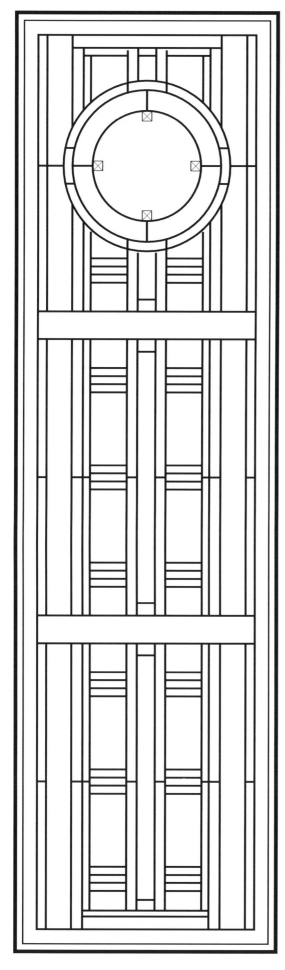

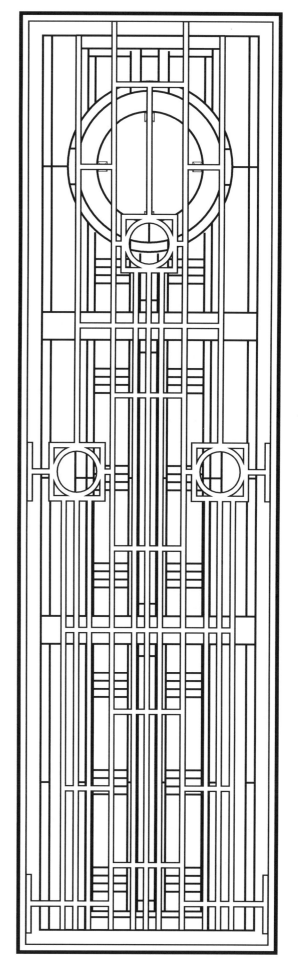

△   □

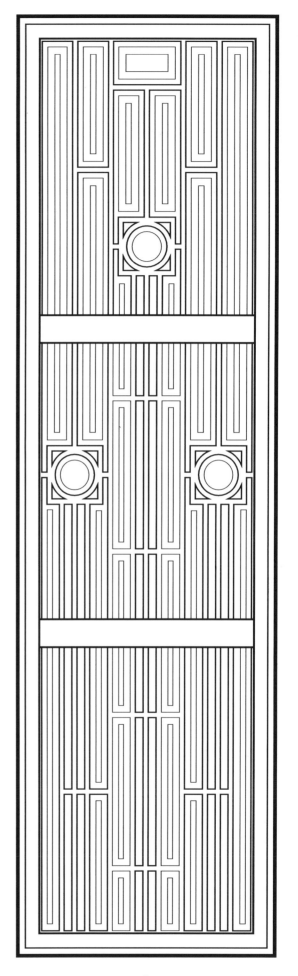

ABA NIGERIA TEMPLE

ASUNCIÓN PARAGUAY TEMPLE

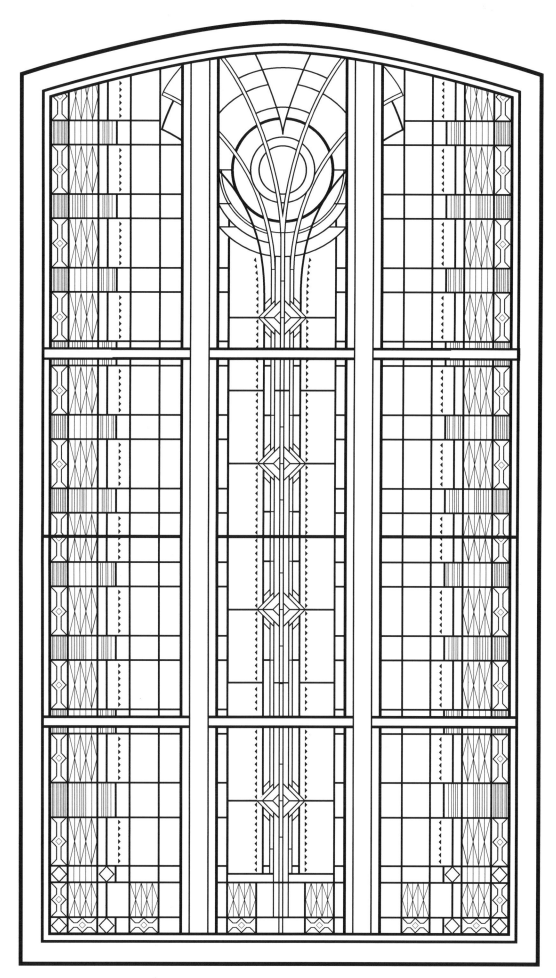

ACCRA GHANA TEMPLE

ALBUQUERQUE NEW MEXICO TEMPLE

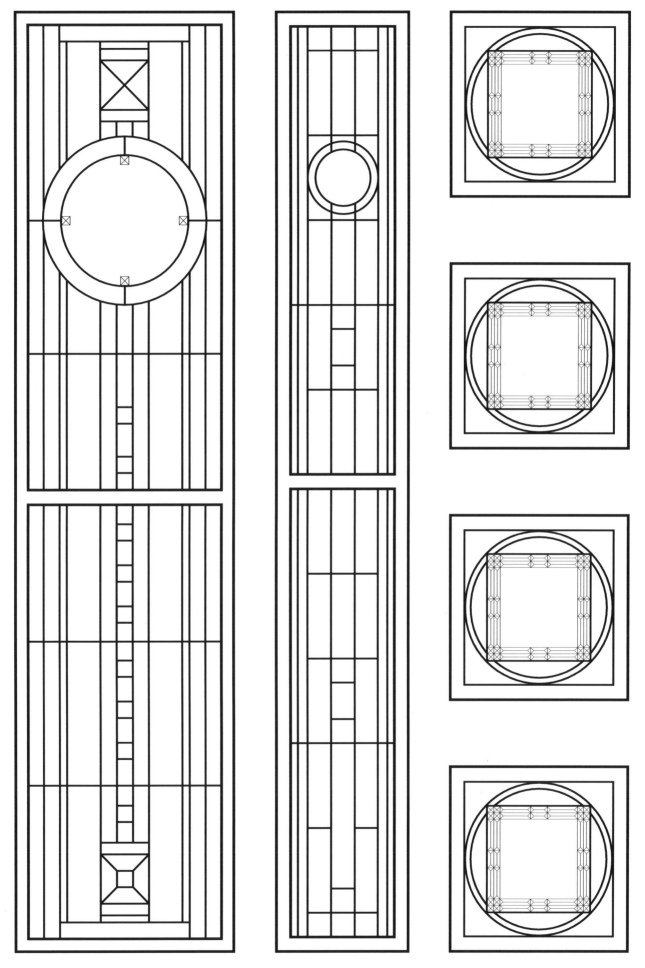

ANCHORAGE ALASKA TEMPLE   MONTICELLO UTAH TEMPLE

APIA SAMOA TEMPLE

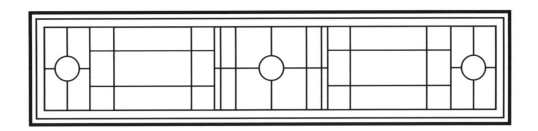

ATLANTA GEORGIA TEMPLE

BERN SWITZERLAND

HAMILTON
NEW ZEALAND

IDAHO FALLS
IDAHO

LOS ANGELES
CALIFORNIA

STOCKHOLM SWEDEN

BERN SWITZERLAND TEMPLE

JOHANNESBURG SOUTH AFRICA

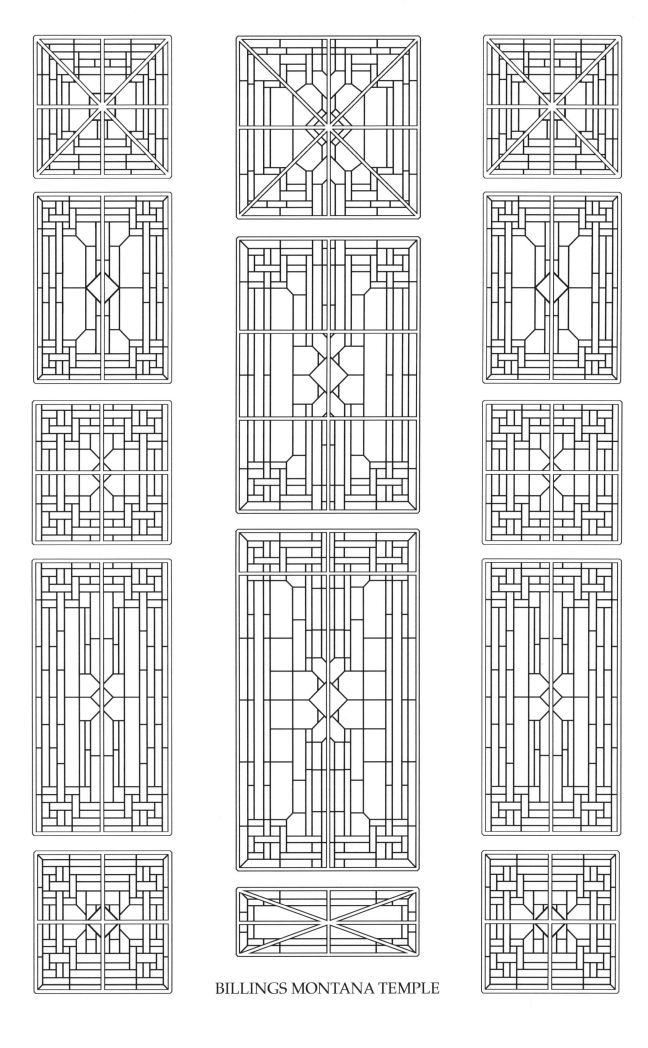

BILLINGS MONTANA TEMPLE

BOGOTÁ COLOMBIA TEMPLE

BOISE IDAHO TEMPLE

BOISE IDAHO TEMPLE

BOSTON MASSACHUSETTS TEMPLE

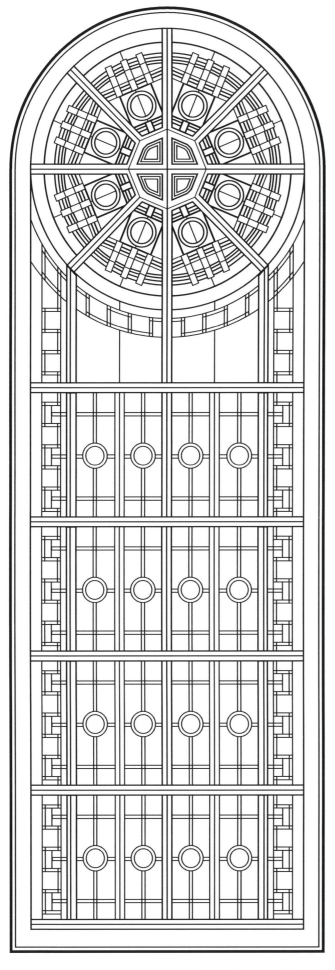

BOUNTIFUL UTAH TEMPLE

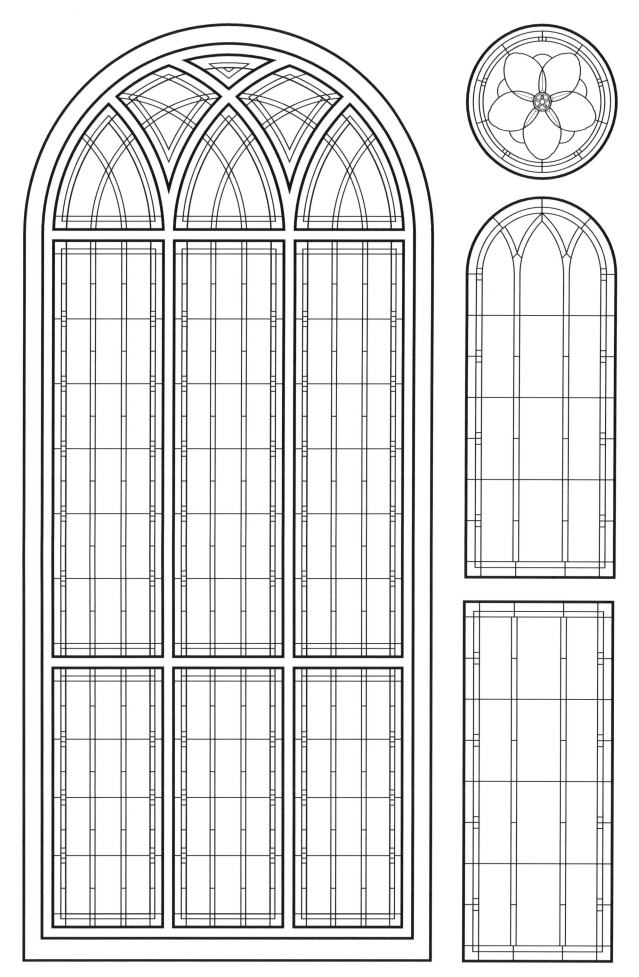

BRIGHAM CITY UTAH TEMPLE

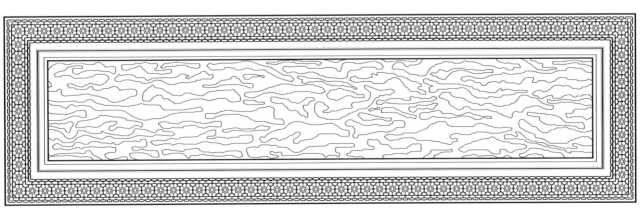

SUVA FIJI TEMPLE

SNOWFLAKE ARIZONA

HONG KONG CHINA

BRISBANE AUSTRALIA

CALGARY ALBERTA TEMPLE

CAMPINAS BRAZIL TEMPLE

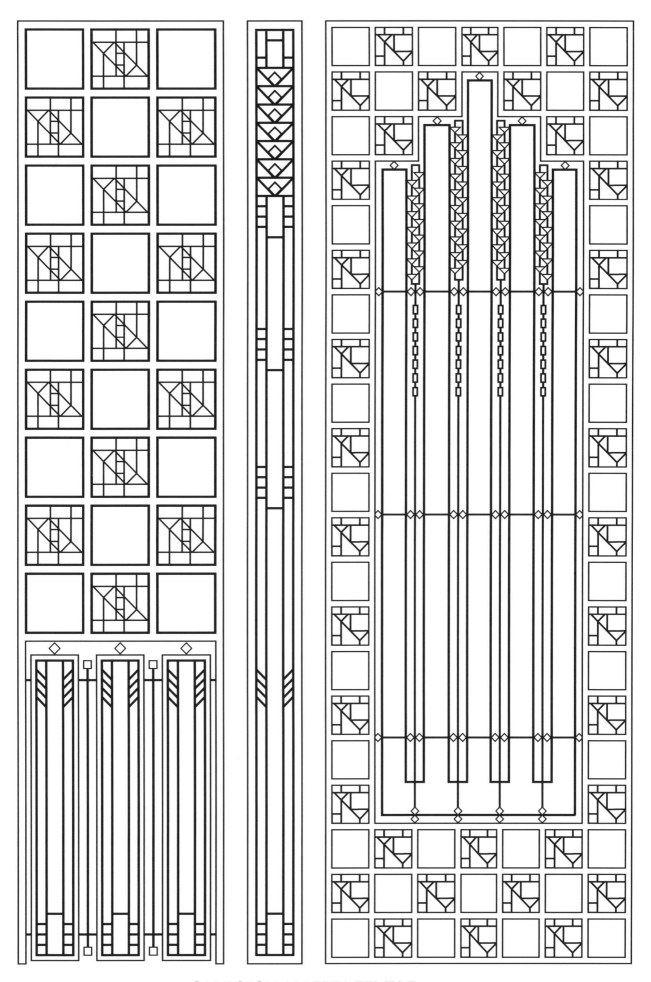

CARDSTON ALBERTA TEMPLE

CEBU CITY PHILIPPINES TEMPLE

CEDAR CITY UTAH TEMPLE   COCHABAMBA BOLIVIA TEMPLE

COLONIA JUÁREZ
CHIHUAHUA MEXICO TEMPLE

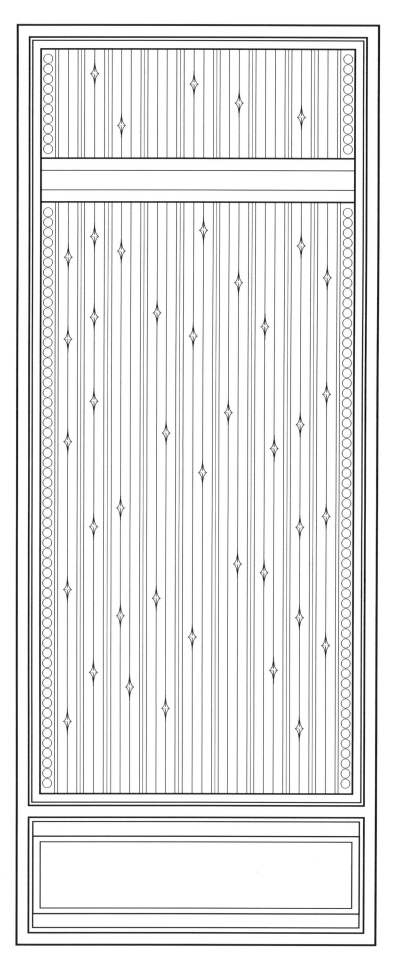

OQUIRRH MOUNTAIN UTAH TEMPLE

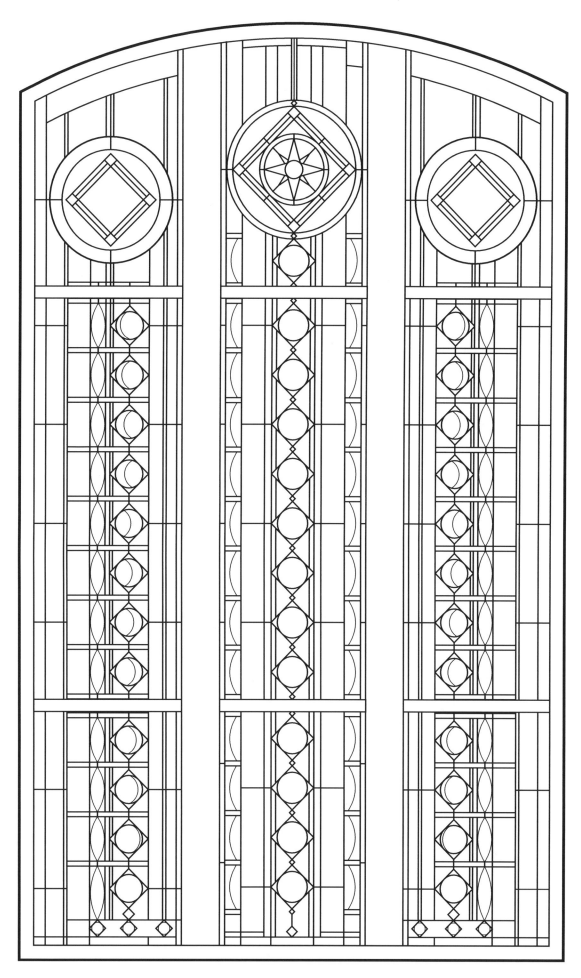

COLUMBIA RIVER WASHINGTON TEMPLE

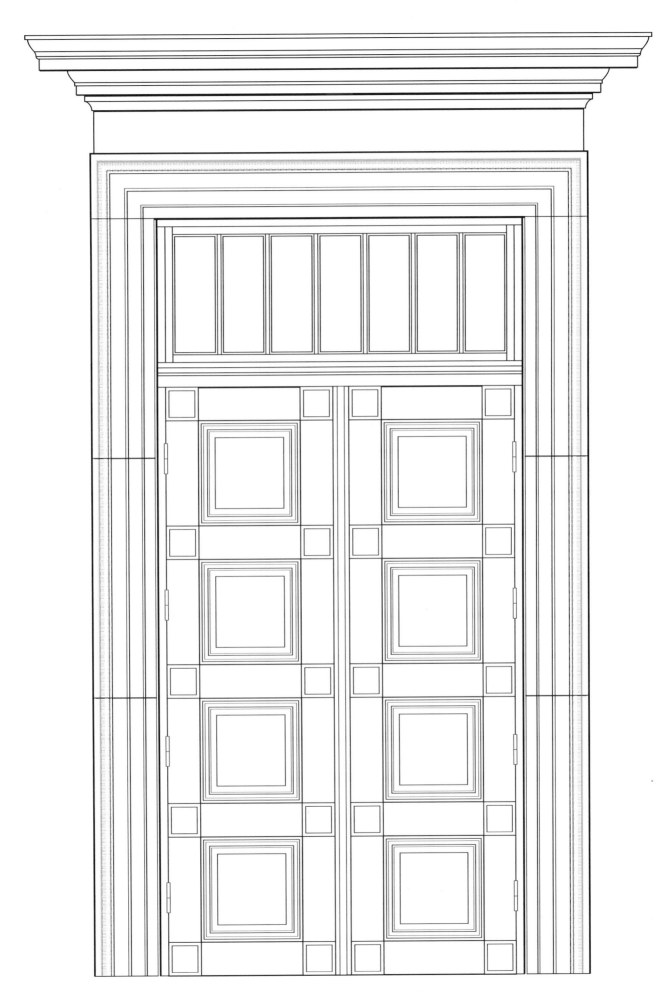

COPENHAGEN DENMARK TEMPLE

CÓRDOBA ARGENTINA TEMPLE

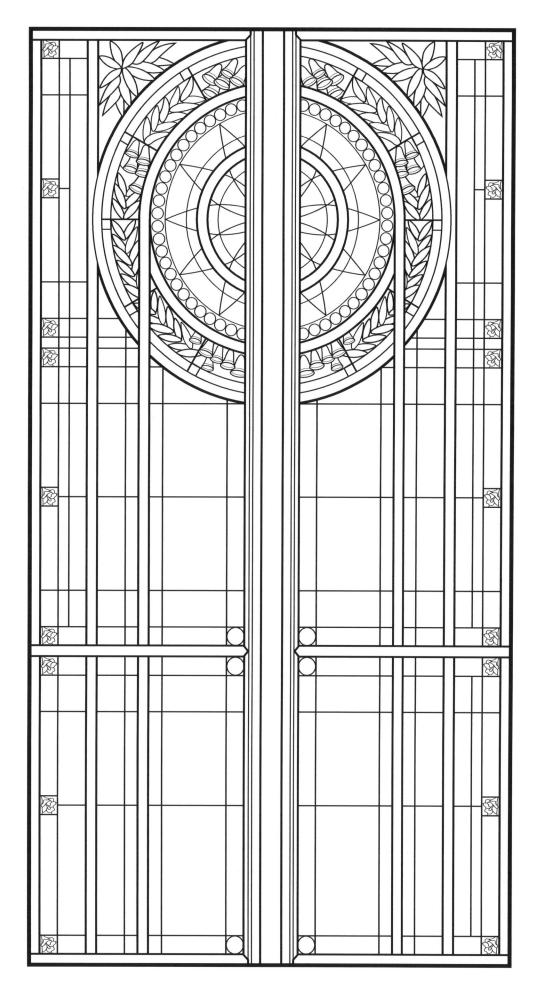

CURITIBA BRAZIL TEMPLE

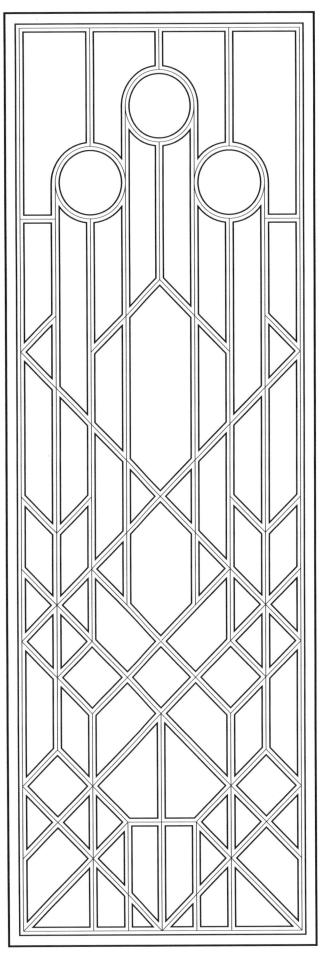

CHICAGO ILLINOIS TEMPLE   DALLAS TEXAS TEMPLE

DENVER COLORADO TEMPLE

DRAPER UTAH TEMPLE

FORT COLLINS COLORADO TEMPLE

FORT LAUDERDALE FLORIDA TEMPLE

FRANKFURT GERMANY TEMPLE   FREIBERG GERMANY TEMPLE

FREIBERG GERMANY TEMPLE

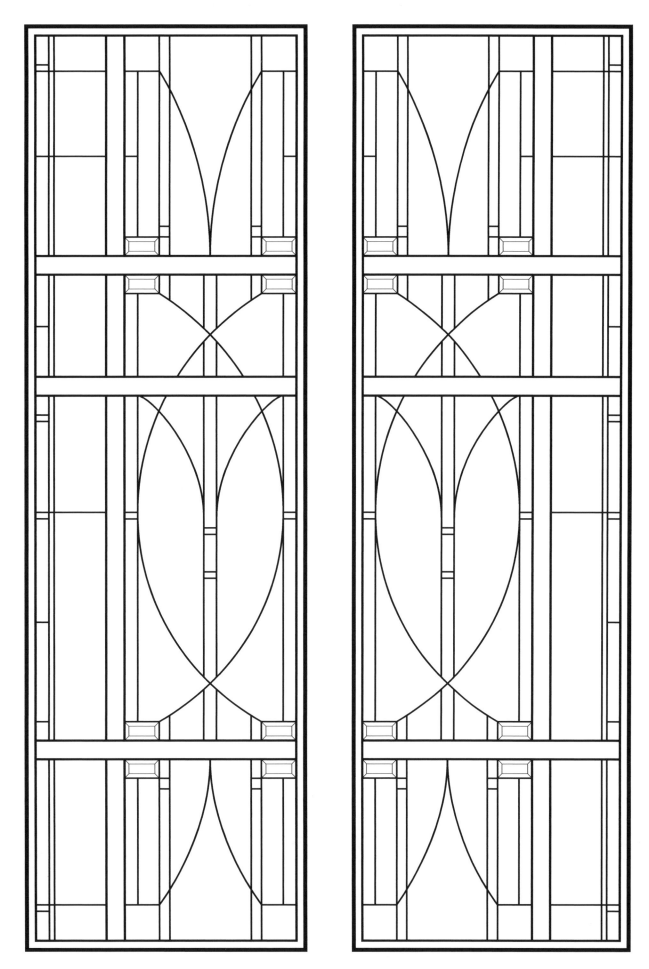

THE GILA VALLEY ARIZONA TEMPLE

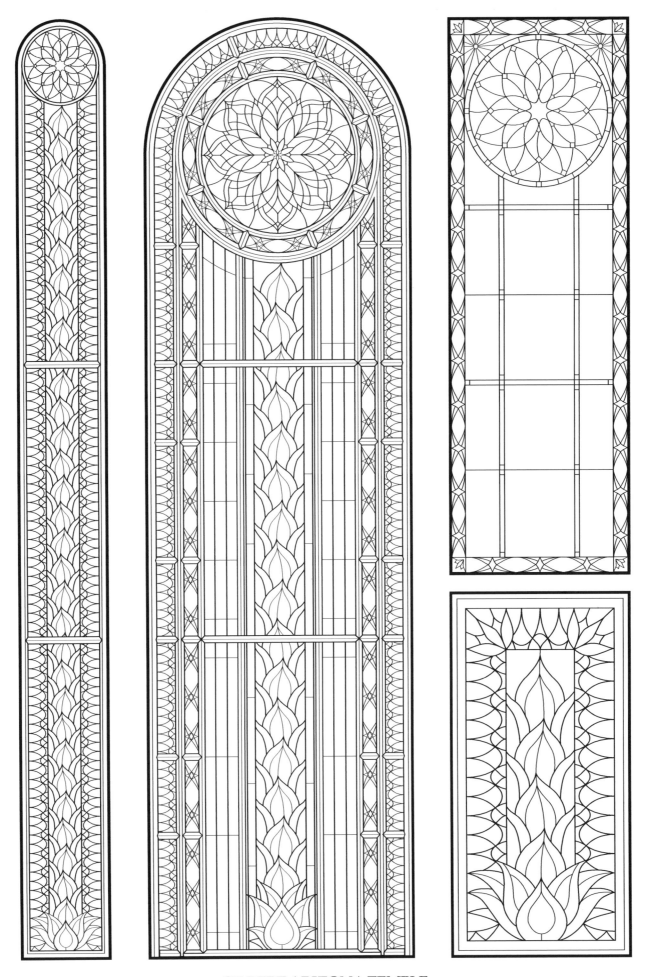

GILBERT ARIZONA TEMPLE

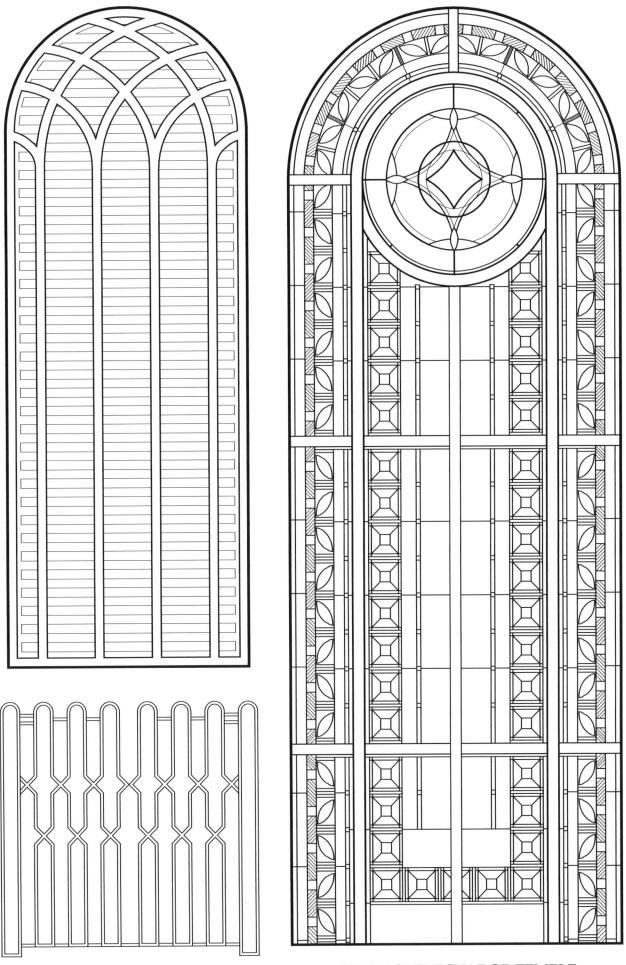

GUATEMALA CITY TEMPLE   GUAYAQUIL ECUADOR TEMPLE

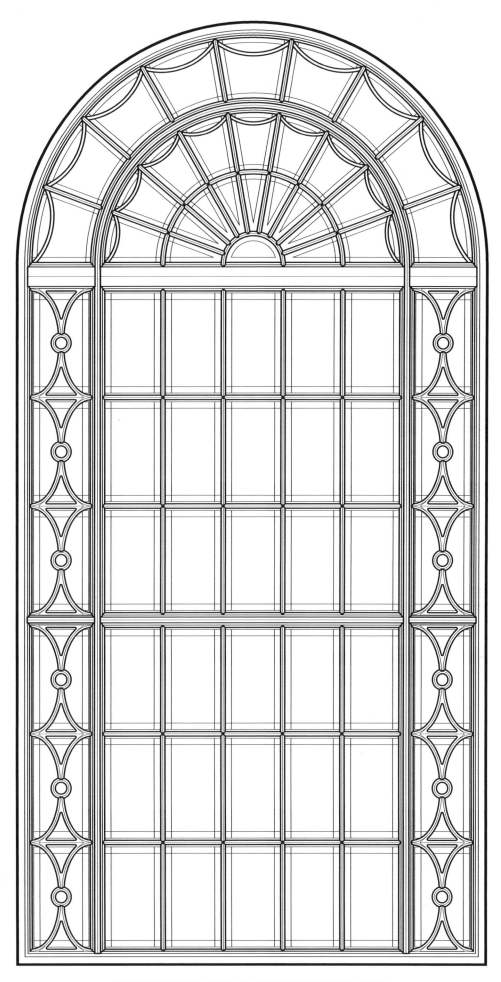

HARTFORD CONNECTICUT TEMPLE

HELSINKI FINLAND TEMPLE

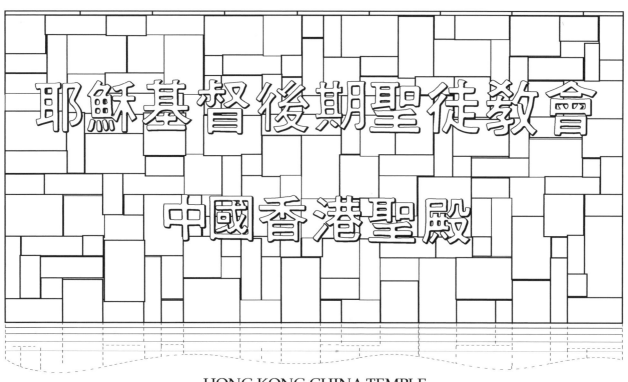

耶穌基督後期聖徒教會

中國香港聖殿

HONG KONG CHINA TEMPLE

HOUSTON TEXAS TEMPLE

IDAHO FALLS IDAHO TEMPLE

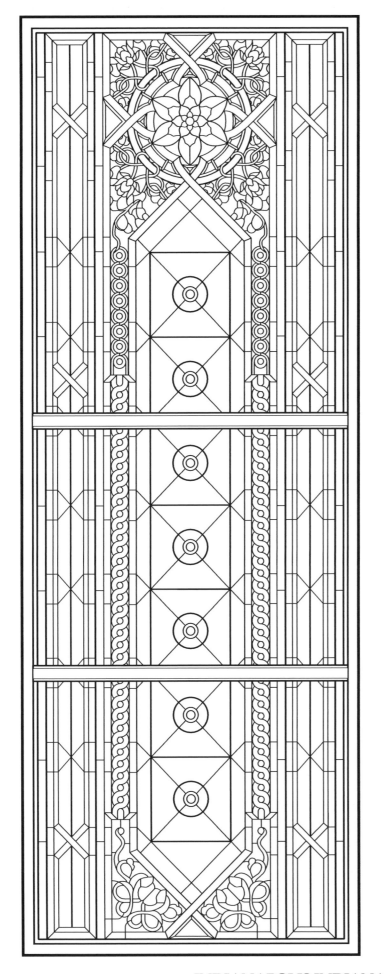

INDIANAPOLIS INDIANA TEMPLE

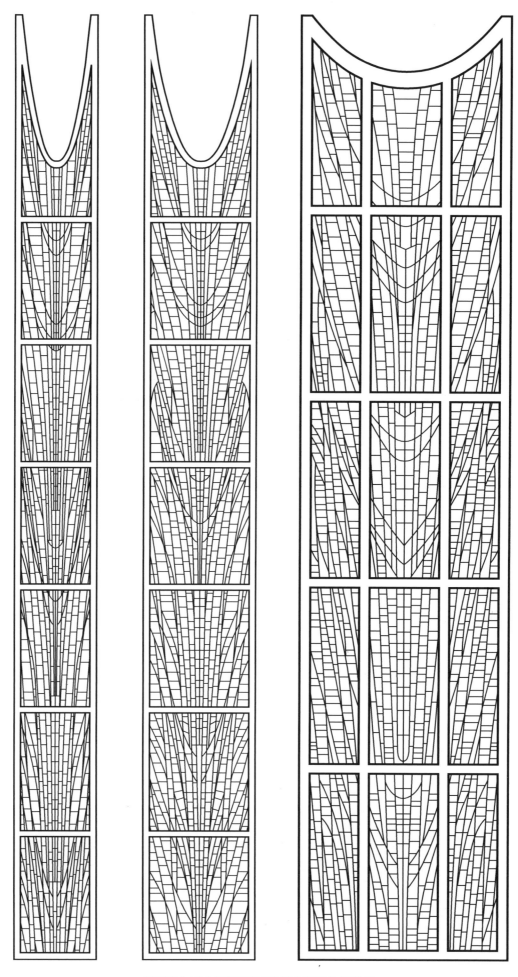

JORDAN RIVER UTAH TEMPLE

KANSAS CITY MISSOURI TEMPLE

KYIV UKRAINE TEMPLE

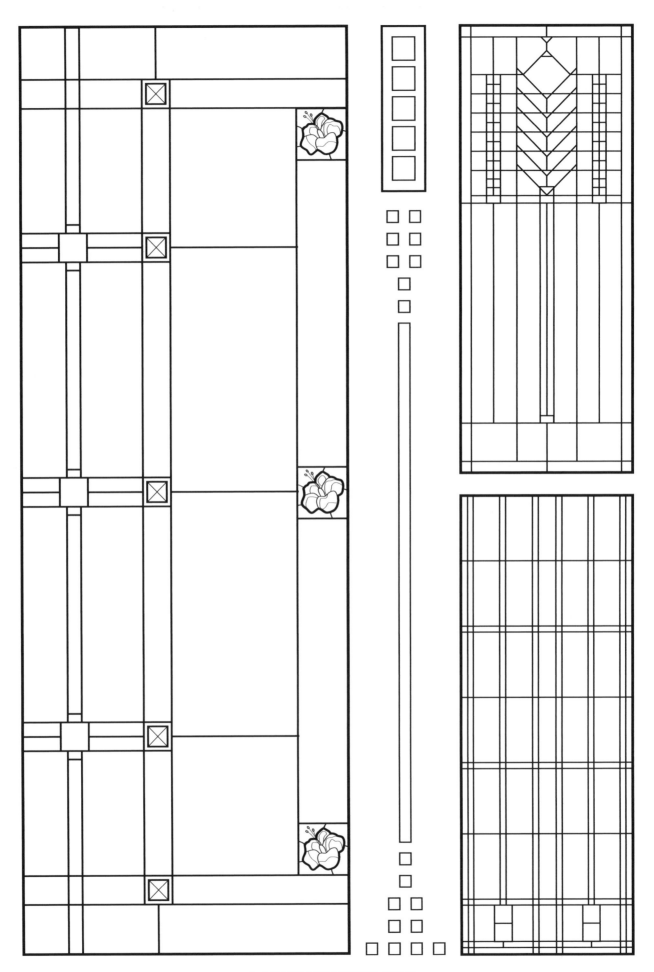

LAIE HAWAII TEMPLE

LAS VEGAS NEVADA TEMPLE

LIMA PERU TEMPLE

LOGAN UTAH TEMPLE

LONDON ENGLAND TEMPLE

LOS ANGELES CALIFORNIA TEMPLE

LUBBOCK TEXAS TEMPLE